I have edited Clive Gilson's boo~~ks for over a decade now, he's~~
prolific and can turn his hand
fiction, contemporary novels, fol
common theme is that none of
away. There's something in eac
poignant, hauntingly unnerving c

GW01072099

Lorna Howarth, *The Write Factor*

Out Of The Walled Garden

-

Selected poetry from the anthology years

Clive Gilson

Out Of The Walled Garden by Clive Gilson, Solitude, Bath, UK

www.boyonabench.com

First published as an eBook in 2018

This edition © 2021 Clive Gilson

Printed by IngramSpark

ISBN: 978-1-913500-38-2

SOLITUDE

Contents

PREFACE

All of these poems have appeared in magazines and anthologies published between 2001 and 2011. Although I did produce an earlier, less inclusive edition of *Out Of The Walled Garden* a few years ago, this new edition includes all of my previously published pieces.

I've largely neglected these poems for the last decade. After the death of my late wife, Karen, in 2010, I lost the heart to continue working in this vein, but now, putting this collection together properly, I've finally found a little of that lost enthusiasm.

As I've worked through each piece, I've also put together some brief notes about the background or thoughts associated with the poem, and I think that this jogging of old memories is important. Over time we lose sight of the people that we once were, traveling further from our source, leaving a trail that slowly becomes overgrown with the weeds of forgetfulness, and we should, I think, try to keep our paths clear so that we can, if we choose to, retrace a few of our steps.

Over the summer I edited a memoir that my father wrote before memory loss took its toll on his abilities, and I wonder, perhaps, if that has made me feel a little nostalgic. If that is the case, then I'm glad of it. It's been good to reminisce and revisit old thoughts. Some of these thoughts and memories are, of course, painful, but in working on these poems I think that some of those sharper points have become a little duller.

It's actually been fun, and I'm all for that.

Clive

Bath, 2021

Arif's Legs

I spent some time in India in the early 1990s, with a short stay around Panjim and Calangute, a few hours south of Mumbai. I remember ordering a coffee in a bar beside a restaurant and watching as newly arrived, fantastic western princes, dressed in bright football allegiances, got their first taste of the country.

Flip-flops smack hard baked sand,

a rhythmic chattering

beneath the soft glide of cheap silk sarongs

and ludicrously loud beach shirts.

Cracked earth and spare weeds

line a path that winds beside bare tables

in the yawning morning shadows

of a Nepalese restaurant.

Arif swings out of the shade

and waits in the sun on a corner.

He squats, smiling, in the company of mangy mongrels,

lounging the day away, waiting for half-finished meals

and overflowing bins at dusk.

In the down draught of beer guts and sweat

Arif's limbs jut and break at right angles.

He crawls on one bent leg,

propelled forwards by one smashed and twisted arm.

His left-hand bends impossibly backwards.

His right arm, his good arm, is raised,

palm upwards and creased with dirt.

Flint brown eyes glint as he grins

from under the spindle bower,

where dogs scratch their baked arses

and the crusting sores behind their ears.

Arif waits, counting the slap of fat foot falls,

preparing to barb his glorious smile.

Seeing colours emerge from the heat haze,

Arif shuffles out onto the path.

He slices sunbeams with his smile,

and knowing the many colours of money,

declares his eternal love

for Manchester United.

At One Blow

For Gerhart Riegner

"Received alarming report that in Fuhrer's headquarters plans discussed and under consideration according to which all Jews in countries occupied or controlled by Germany numbering 3½ - 4 millions should after deportation and concentration in the East be exterminated at one blow to resolve once and for all the Jewish Question in Europe"

From a telegram sent to London & Washington by Gerhart Riegner in August 1942 containing a report on the Wannsee Conference, January 1942.

Yellow paper, annotated,

the surface barely scratched,

broken codes, confusion,

evidence ignored, insubstantial,

too few to witness,

and tired with the effort of making war,

of moulding a new world in the shape

of this blitzed collective act of will,

there is a comment:

"A rather wild story".

BALANCING MIXED VEGETABLES ON A MOTORWAY BRIDGE

Fergus McTaggart was someone I knocked about with for a spell while at university in Leeds. We shared a house. Fergus was a little older than the rest of us and he loved the craic... especially when he could provoke a wee reaction. I was, of course, one of the boys.

Fergus vomits a little in the street.

Walking to the pub he stops

and deposits bile in the gutter.

"Better out..." he says.

Fergus walks miles out of his way

to find a bridge over the ring road

and, urged on by boys who admire

the calculated insanity of the man,

he climbs onto the safety rail

and walks backwards with his eyes shut.

None of the boys can tear their eyes

away from roadkill fascination.

Fergus shouts and cracks a smile.

The boys grin and shout back,

in thrall to the image of a body

lying fifty feet below them.

The trick is being in control,

balancing the weight of possibility

against the boy's lack of imagination.

The boys are sick in the gutter,

depositing small rivers of Tetley's

finest ale down the drains.

BURNING BOOKS

This one came, I think, from a short film reel from pre-war Germany that made me think about burning away thoughts, letter by letter...

At four hundred and fifty-one degrees Fahrenheit

crisply charred letters fall like snowflakes,

perfect crystalline structures.

Black windows glitter diamond spots of light

where sparks dribble across the night.

Each floating ember is a letter,

a burning flicker of inspiration

falling to earth, fading and dying

on cold, hard ground.

Feverish tongues lick spines,

curling through bindings,

obscuring sense and sentiment,

unravelling logic and argument,

laughing at a lover's pains

and life's raw comedy.

Stanzas weep.

Chapters suffocate.

Somewhere, out there

at the edge of the fire glow,

a new page is set alight

and the story starts again

from the beginning.

COURTYARD

A few years ago, I adapted this piece as a short story. I've always had a soft spot for this poem. I think the inspiration is wrapped up in my imagined scenery from Gormenghast, Mervyn Peake being a genius of the very highest order.

With the sun at his back

he follows his shadow

across herringbone paviours

pitted by frost and chipped by ice,

worn smooth by boot heels.

Each brick was placed

by calloused hands,

butted against a neighbour,

crisp and clean, a geometrically

arranged enclosure.

The sun sweeps the sky,

a new broom, bright and bristling,

and stones weather and fade,

dull but not colourless

under brilliant blue brush strokes.

His eyes fix on a point of perspective,

above the patterns beneath his feet.

Each stone, individually set out,

imagined and roughly mapped,

is a monument to craft and guile.

The walker, focused, wrapped up

In the artificial fibres that form

end-of-year bottom line errands

and corporate reporting, walks on,

blissfully unaware of the plan beneath his feet,

laid down with hard skin, blisters and scars.

GHOST LIES IN LIGHT

Talking of Mervyn Peake, this is another piece that is definitely rooted in Titus Groan. At the time of editing this piece I've not read Gormenghast for a few years, but I think the beetle is a direct lift from the original. In the spirit of retracing steps along life's path I have just resolved to order a new copy of the book...

An eye blinks beneath a veil

of splayed pine branches

and the sleeper awakes

where gaunt, blown limbs

wrap themselves in knots.

Purple dawn soaks into

the stiff sinews of the night.

He stretches his legs.

His breath is shallow

and he dare not brush

a pine needle from its place

in case the dead flex

their bleached white hands.

The sleeper stifles a cough.

By his knee, scrabbling

towards him, sparkling

emerald under the last

of the fading moonbeams

a beetle absorbs black sky,

and casts a shadow across

his leg, a presence at odds

with its miniature existence.

HESPERUS WRECKED

Koufonissia is a stunning little Greek island. My late wife and I visited for a number of years, quietly sipping our way through wine and Metaxa. This was written on our first visit, when we stayed in a small apartment owned by Mister Cucumberi. That's what we called him because every morning he left a fresh cucumber and a large tomato for us on the patio table.

Pastels, deep flowing blues, long hours,

sunlight through closed shutters,

incandescence streaming into the room,

an evening star, summer night perspiration,

fingers at play, sparring with shadows,

dog-day heat, when the world grows quiet,

oppressed, brazier red under cloudless heights,

swooning with the sway of dry edged palms,

borne on the effervescent Meltemi;

In these hours, breathless bodies lay prone,

panting, tender, bathed in sweat, peeling skin.

They shift the tangled sheets from around their feet.

They are laced together, her legs astride his groin,

her head on his chest, and she sighs softly,

inhaling rapidly, tracing the contours

of his spent muscles with the tips

of her own exhausted fingers

in the quiet space between them,

where children's voices drift on the wind

and the bleat of a solitary goat tethers

the harsh white moon, he holds her tightly,

enclosed in the drowse dead minutes

marked by the run of tears falling

across her cheek, mingling with the sweat

they are bathed in.

She looks up and smiles, iris wide and deep,

and hazel-blue is the colour of love beneath

wet eyelashes blinking in the silence,

in the heat of the night,

in the light of blue louvered shadows,

and he is the first to break,

a joke;

she looks like the "Wreck of the Hesperus"

LENA'S PARTING GIFTS

I pulled a few family stories together over the years and this is one of them. Lena was my mother's favourite aunt. She lived with Lena when she first came down to London from Yorkshire in the 1950s and they remained close until Lena's death. This story combines some early memories of mine with one of my mother's recollections

Trees hang low, their sodden branches

weighed down by teardrops,

glistening under iron skies.

Drip by drip a scale model railway track,

built on four courses of crumble-edged house bricks,

rusts away to thin brittle flakes,

and wheel-clacks are remembered

without substance, where the trees hang.

Overgrown, the autumn washed pinks

of straggling Lavatera blow west with the wind

that carries shallow bottomed grey-heads

over these slip-shod, rattle-tiled roofs.

Tendrils scratch their needle fingers

across long forgotten dirt smeared windows

where the trees hang.

Faint reds reflect on wet sliced flagstones

whose black edges soak in towards their centres,

the unswept stain of dry summer earth

trapped in rain heavy grass.

In the mirror shapes of a tall suburb

the sound of faint but constant water falls

where the trees hang.

Behind glass, spattered with opaque splashes,

sat on hard wearing crimson cloth,

earnest voices whisper, respecting dear memory,

but firing hoarsely nonetheless.

Whipping words declare that they were the ones

who should have the green model engine

that ran on the tracks where the trees hang.

Eyes strain. Some of the mourners

shape keepsakes for love,

others for the value in the object.

Sitting or standing,

looking out onto the path,

where the Lavatera blows west

and red bricks merge into wet reflections,

fingers tap and elbows nudge under a bare bulb,

the shade already gone to a good home

where trees stand in the rain

and hang their heavy heads.

MOLLIE SMOKES PLAYERS

Mary Olive Carter (Mollie) was my maternal grandmother. So many memories from a lovely lady, but this is one of the perennial images that comes to me when I think of her.

Chromed pixie,

lid of a biscuit barrel,

grimy with little fingerprints,

trapping dust in sculpted folds,

an old Bush radio, Bakelite knobs

etched with cream spots, a string

drawn tuner fluttering uncertainly

between Moscow, the Light Programme

and the centre of the room,

where, cold and clinker drab,

a pot belly stove sits like a castle.

Standing by a heavy electric cooker,

a Belling, in a pale blue housecoat,

her back to the room, staring

out of a window at drizzle

and glossy bitumen-black roofs,

Mollie lays a wooden mixing spoon on the hob.

A cigarette hangs from her lip,

ash curving downwards with gravity.

We're having mince and dead tobacco for tea,

but then she cups her hand, catches the ash,

drops it into the dolly-paunched stove,

turns, lights another unfiltered Players ciggie,

and says something about making the bed.

The cigarette glows as ash forms,

starting its downward arc once again,

and picking up the wooden spoon,

she stirs the mince and onions

in time to the beat of Barry Ryan's

longing for Eloise.

Mollie is lost in music and grandchildren.

Ash falls.

ROSES REMEMBERED

Whisky, log fires and late night attempts to put the world to rights. For a while there we were close friends, but things rarely remain constant and I certainly played my part in things going awry. I remember those nights fondly, though.

They hung upside down,

their fading pinks and

ragged edges brittle

in the rising fire's draft.

They hung, dry as dust,

wrapped in gold silk,

pinned to salt leeched bricks

black with smoky evenings.

Beech logs, dust piled,

stacked away the spider webs

in a splintered corner,

where once we gazed quietly on,

as the Christians waited to burn.

In those ember warm nights

when spaniels slept contentedly,

we talked away the hours,

cupping in our hands a world

that tumbled through the glowing gauze

of Grouse and flame.

Building Chinon,

stone by heavy stone,

Eleanor and Henry and Richard

wormed their way

through worlds of words.

John Barry strode across a tired sky,

thundering the night blacks

with themes describing giants.

Magicians spun the world around,

breaking the backs of penitents,

cracking the spines of sinners,

until some new dawn flew in across

the dry tongued creak of empty heads

and pin holed, armchair bones.

In the haze of smoking guns,

we saved lost boys and,

as the years rolled on,

sang for forty shillings on the drum.

A time of roses,

spilling green remembered leaves

upon the passing hours.

There were scratches of vapour

trailing cross the dawn blue sky

as we looked up from our crying game.

Behind us, the ragged lip

decayed a little more

and dropped its curve,

its shallow hue,

onto sooty tiles

and faded, finally,

into pale, spent

ash and dust.

THE MAN WHO LOVES COMETS

This was, I think, the first of the cancer poems. My late wife, Karen, was diagnosed with breast cancer in early 2006. Her battle with Trevor (we named her tumour so that we could come to terms with the whole thing. It was easier to curse Trevor than some amorphous growth.) involved the full course of treatments and I wrote this one evening, sat in our bedroom as Karen struggled with the side-effects from her chemotherapy.

When sleep leaves him the artex on the ceiling spirals

and the night dark spins above his head as she,

the slow revolving maelstrom, snores and groans,

beached on her side, her back towards him.

Lifting the duvet with a care that comes

from watching the dead by candle light,

he rises without sound, like flowing mercury,

and eases open a bedroom window to gaze at sky.

Surrounded by dense, emphatic slumber

and the endless orbit of the draining board,

feeling like a little boy in ragged shorts,

he flies abreast solar winds, catching at dragon tails.

The maelstrom moves in her sleep

on a creak of well-worn bedsprings,

a viscose, fluid, phlegmy creature,

far removed from the brusque,

daylight creator of love-drowned days.

He turns his eyes upon her face,

a pale and sagging moon,

and he forgets his streaming satellite.

His feet are cold. He shuts the window,

pads across the hoovered carpet

and weighs the value of life

in these lonely waking hours.

ANGEL FALLS

We were watching a stage adaptation of Lord Of The Flies at the Oxford Playhouse in 2002, I think, and out of the corner of my eye I thought I saw a movement at the front of the circle balcony. The play was excellent, but I did find the image slightly disconcerting, and it lead to this

A boy sits on a stage,

the words he delivers rising clearly.

He is bathed in yellow filtered spotlights.

Drifts of lazy smoke catch the beam

as it widens, encircling the boy,

whose knees are drawn up to his chin.

He rests his back against a steel frame.

At the periphery of my vision, I see an Angel,

standing perfectly still, waxed and pallid,

balancing upon the Circle balustrade.

The brass rail gleams along its forward edge,

reflecting the lights from the stage.

I cannot see this creature's colours.

I see just a plain shape.

Angel's arms hang straight down by his side,

and his gaze is fixed and forward.

The boy speaks of simple things,

of quiet home where order lay.

The boy pauses mid-sentence…

The light filters white…

Angel raises his arms above his head,

languid, mercury flowing in glass,

flawless in liquid execution.

Angel moves his arms to the perpendicular

and lets his body drift down on simple gravity,

pivoting forward on his feet as if diving

into the dead-calm pool of the stalls.

The spotlight cuts to black.

Bodies in shadow take new positions on the stage.

People fidget and cough.

BREAKFAST WITH AUDREY

Another Greek island, slightly hungover, having a late breakfast with Karen, yoghurt and honey and omelettes, I think, with thick black coffee. For some reason the moment made me think of Audrey Hepburn.

Honey drips onto fingers holding bread

that soaks up slow, golden, sweetness.

Coffee cups rattle down to the bitters

and a half-eaten omelette grows cold

in a thick sea of tomato sauce.

Bright white crockery catches brilliant sunlight.

In these early hours, when bars and cafes lay dormant,

at one with the boozy sloth of happy travellers,

the heat drips.

On a balcony, shaded from slow sun time,

wrapped in white cotton and dark glasses,

her soft, elegant hand holds a glass

of freshly squeezed orange juice,

dribbling condensation.

She sits quietly beneath acrylic angels,

framed for bleary eyes and bored waiters.

She looks like a blonde Audrey Hepburn,

laughing sweetly at the state I'm in.

Looking out from the shadows on the balcony,

out under clear, soaring skies of endless blue,

the Chrysanthemums blossom just for me,

the deepest red that I've ever seen.

LLANARROW

A quiet moment sat in soft lamplight in a rented cottage at Llanarrow. This was a brief interlude on one of our annual weekends scouring the second-hand bookshops at Hay-On-Wye.

The evening hours of spring spill into lamplight.

Mud on trouser bottoms flakes onto beige panelled patterns,

where she sits, curled up on the sofa.

She has wrapped herself around my arm, nesting,

blending in with the shadow cast by my book, read warmly.

Time drifts into lapsed conversation,

while John Tavener rains thunder,

mixing with red wine, breathing.

She stirs, burrowing deeper, easier with minutes

and the floating lace veil through which we glimpse ourselves.

These, for me, are the easiest days,

safe in blues and browns and tired eyes.

This is the forever of shared humours

sitting lightly on these thick stone walls,

where a clock shuffles the day down.

A BROKEN HEART

We spent a lot of time hanging around in hospital corridors in the late 2000s. This piece came out of a visit to Cheltenham where I often spent time waiting and watching people as they too dealt with their own stresses during a loved one's illness.

She was beautiful, a homespun bonny,

warm in bed and sharp on life's edge,

quick witted and funny, hard as a diamond,

a dissolving cascade of soft pillow comfort.

When he came home drunk on a Friday night,

beery with boys' tales and smoking with love,

she used to raise her eyebrows, sit him down,

scold him and then nestle into the warmth

of his arms.

A simple thing, this partnership,

this life, ordinary amongst the vast scale,

a parlour game, a soap sud procession,

but never a crossed word, never anger.

He sinks to his knees, waterlogged,

his right hand gripping the flesh above

his failing heart.

That morning, in the washroom light

of another early September day,

he found her on the kitchen floor.

He cradled her until harsh blue lights spun.

This evening, as she lay in the wired,

respirator tube aftermath of cardiac arrest,

the learned leeches came,

dark in eye, with nervous fingers,

anxious to comfort

but unsure how to touch,

to say that she wouldn't see the dawn again.

The space in which he stands,

an antiseptic, green painted room,

assumes the weightless nature of water,

the unseen liquid rising without a ripple

across his chest and into his mouth, nose and eyes.

His breathing ceases.

He falls in slow motion, watching the days

of his life drown with him.

He falls forwards.

Linoleum is the last thing he sees.

BLIND MAN BATHING

Taking a bath during a power outage at the farm in Devon. The whole experience was slightly freaky, and later I developed this piece as a short story called Wind Freaks.

Distance is measured with the tap of white wood,

a brass ferule on a skirting board, a step,

a motion forward in the dark, a level playing field,

walled, straight and long with open doors pegged back,

the frame and architrave a moment, architectural,

the trigonometry of space and living applied, a cosine,

a living depth that defines the metre of this universe,

this expression, this line, this place of undressing.

Clothes drop to the floor,

a rumpled hill of cotton and wool,

a soiled shirt collar laying down with belt and braces.

A hand stretches out, soft skin brushing enamel tenderly.

Spreading fingers search for water, testing, flexing,

assessing heat and size, a deepness of sound, silent fathoms.

A foot lifts, hanging, naked, an anklebone catches

on metal, scratching calcium and protein,

a white mark on skin.

A drawing of breath, a step into water,

Hotter than the fingers imagined

in scales of familiarity and use,

one leg, two legs, the smoothness of tiles on palms,

the sinking of knees, the resting of elbows on hard,

iron castings, cold still but warming through.

A body slides down, heat rising across a stomach,

water sliding over folds of flesh, breaking over breasts,

lights on and a full stream of darkness rising,

the foetal sack envelops, slides up to chin and jowl.

Reaching behind his head, his hair curling-damp,

sweat beading his forehead, his body swelling in heat,

glowing, steam-pink, a bottle is moved, and another,

a plastic chamber piece plays, scratching grout and silicone,

shapes tumble under worm wriggling, nervous fingers,

skin slips and slimes on the rime ring of white water edges.

There is a call, a hallway rush of air and voice,

a loss of place, motion in black space,

a resignation, a wait, a grain of understanding.

Someone, some person unseen, has moved the shampoo.

BOYS IN SUMMER

I saw a couple of pictures at my mother and father's flat, pictures showing my father, Leslie, in a couple of laddish poses with the old Brentford gang that he grew into manhood with. I've subsequently archived a host of these old photographs, and always smile when I see these two sepia holiday snaps.

A picture, an Eastman Kodak print,

six by four, smudged and corner bent,

shows four boys, late teens, on a beach,

sun kissed, salt tangled, rib thin,

patched with pink speckled sunburn

and beery, bloodshot eyes that grin,

a last hurrah before the weary tread

of work and college and forgetting.

In a drawer, discovered rummaging,

four boys, twenty-something lads,

who kicked tin cans down bombed out streets,

stand, arms around each other's shoulders,

in grey fade shades, with heavy hair,

all duck's arse and cocky swagger,

bumped by the train to Brighton

for a stick of rock and a good time girl

at the Palais, a walk-you-home

and a goodnight kiss.

Most of the boys have gone,

bread floating on a millpond sea,

saturating and sinking.

A mind wanders the sands,

wondering if the pictures taken

by boys on the beach,

forgotten these twenty years,

will be joined by the hopeful fizz

of digital sons and daughters,

taking their own memory snaps

in the sunlight-blue of an Ibiza dawn,

laying the trail that runs

through the short days of brief lives.

CHAIRS REMEMBER TOO

We had a thoroughly worn green Chesterfield in the living room down on the Devon farm, the seats showing clear wear and tear, being dimpled by bottoms over many years. When the time came to replace the seat padding it struck me that we might be losing a whole set of memories.

There is a shape to a chair,

to the skeleton frame and the slow rise

of covers and weight worn stuffing.

People fit their favourite chair,

moulding the snug nest of cushion and arm

to their relaxing, to their evenings,

wrapped in the blanket of a book,

lowered inside their sleeping eyes,

or devouring the latest craze on the box.

Conversations drift through days

with bodies draped, at ease,

comfortable in velour and leather folds.

To know a chair by a shape,

by a depth of wearing and to see

a stranger fidget their own comfort

into this piece of familiarity

breaks the common rail

with opposites and contradictions,

different clothes, words and phrases.

But be sure that this seat remembers too,

bearing different weights in silence

and then recovering the well-worn shell

of years and familiar bodies,

listing to port as ever it did.

CLOSING OF THE CHAPEL

I spent a few years treading the boards in and around Oxfordshire, and spent quite a lot of time waiting outside village halls and small local theatres for the person with the keys to come and open up for us. Thame Players had their own theatre, an old chapel, and while waiting one day I got to musing.

Flakes of paint decay under damp moss,

All my hope on God is founded

Grass lies bleeding on a cracked paving stone,

Breathe on me breath of God

Nettle heads rise at the coaxing of weak spring sunlight,

For the beauty of the Earth

Broken glass dances on skeins of carpet thread,

I heard the voice of Jesus say

Weather beaten doors hang on splitting hinges,

Mine eyes have seen the glory

Cast-iron bolts are encased in sarcophagi of rust,

The day thou gavest, Lord, is ended

Plaster cracks with the fading echo of prayerful voices,

There is a green hill far away

A book of hymns blackens with rain fed mildew,

Shall we gather at the river

The fabric of Bethesda is overrun by rats and feral cats,

Guide me, oh thou Great Redeemer

Nailed to a post, a notice witnessing conversion,

Rock of ages

DAISY

Karen and I were attending a wedding in Las Vegas, taking a trip in a convertible Mustang along Route 66 after the main event. This piece came about after a very late night in a bar where we'd fetched up after chatting to a local in a hotel lobby. Karen, as always, was on brilliant form.

A slow rumble of pistons and exhaust baffles,

a Harley growls, rough on mountain air.

Bottles of Budweiser, ice cold,

drip condensation onto denimed legs.

Astride a bench, her shirt tied under her breasts,

teasing the bandana boys with smiles

and big wide eyes, lashes full

on a tide of black mascara,

she baits the bull for a t-shirt,

a "Harley Fuck You",

promising high heels behind wire wheels,

all daisy boots and perfect roots,

all collars and cuffs, but it's …

"Hey boys, he's the one".

Late night limousine headlights in the car park,

high rollers up from Vegas for the early morning mist,

high-top American beauties in search of hard edged

witty shit from behind the bar.

Daisy sits, betting down with valley girls,

all boots and Brummie twang,

swivelling on a chrome laddered stool,

chatting nine to the dozen with every face

that shows the slightest interest in English space.

Daisy pulls dollar bills from her pocket

and dollar bills from the wall,

notes from lovers who called

and nailed their good luck charms on wood,

lost in a weave of cigarette smoke

in the bar's alcoholic half-light haze.

Daisy is watched by lone rangers,

is given "come to bed" looks

by denim cut-offs and pony-tails,

as she scatters herself around the room,

catching eyes and flies in the clear cicada night

amongst these red rock canyon hills.

In a room full of loud talk,

glasses fall empty on wooden tables,

eyes meet, and there is a quiet second,

a moment of recognition,

that says, "Time to go home",

because you see, boys…

"He's the one".

IN FOR THE KILL

Working in the fields on the farm in Devon sometime around 2005, we had a spell of particularly warm weather. This piece was rooted in a summer drowse dream come nightmare. I've often dreamt about predation, from both sides, and rather than being scared of these dreams I've learned to quite enjoy them....

time; the drop of the latch, drowsy poppy heads,

sunlight drone skimming eddies, dark hearts of nectar,

sweeping swallow air, a dry-stone path, daisy feathers

place; a fringed field edge, spotted bramble hedgerows,

a soft sole stumble across dust coughing stones stopped,

silence, absence of birdsong, flies scratching the horizon

predator; calm and level, staring back at me, amber eye,

measurement, a blur stretching, lengthening, shadows,

blood pumping, legs clueless, nightmare swathed

safety; slamming reckless wood, a snarl, carnivorous motion,

summer breath burning, man-eater exhalations, grazed knees,

a deer caught in the baying convergence of dogs and coats

picturesque; waking, skylight, ridge tile dancing,

breathless, at bay, sitting back against a chimney stack,

mesmerised by the dandelion prince pacing the courtyard

INTO THE WALLED GARDEN

Written just after my mother was diagnosed with Parkinsons, and reflects on a conversation that we had in which she felt that her horizons were narrowing and that she would now be bound to take ever smaller steps in the world. She overcame these fears and found different ways to be free.

We end with the worrying gardener,

chiding herself quietly under her breath

with a,"Mary, Mary, not quite so loud, dear".

It wouldn't do to have the neighbours overhear.

She walks on crazily laid paving,

desperate to avoid the twist and turn

of wide angled cracks.

Every step that she takes

is half the length of the previous step.

The shadows cast by brick and mortar

narrow the line of sunlight on the path

with the closing of the hours.

At the bottom of the garden,

down where the Lavatera hangs

heavy with dripping seed heads,

down where the rose hips swell,

is an old ship-lap shed,

feather board patched and cobwebbed,

in the front of which a door hangs ajar.

She has work to do in the dark

with her grubby nails, tender work,

in amongst the smell of dry caked oil

on brittle-stiff bicycle chains

and cans of two-stroke fumes.

She wrings her hands and tangles her fingers,

as she shuffles over stones and yellow flower heads,

drawn in by decaying compost

and dust crusted terracotta pots.

There's work to do, new growth to brew,

but the steps that she takes grow smaller

as does the sweep of the hands

on an old silver pocket watch

in her dressing table drawer.

In a faint but warmly remembered shift of air

brittle sheets of yellow newspaper,

that line dried out baskets

hanging from rust streaked hooks,

rattle like playing cards

in a child's bicycle wheel spokes.

LET'S ALL MOVE TO FRANCE

My late wife Karen and I spent a couple of weeks driving through France in 2004, combining a visit to see Karen's brother, Chris, with visiting some of our favourite places. This piece was inspired by a conversation that I overheard while sitting outside a café underneath the walls of Chinon castle.

Jean Jacques Couasnon

sucks air thought his teeth,

loading the morning

with diligent Gallic charm

and the promise of

a whole new world of wiring.

He clicks his tongue

against the roof of his mouth,

calculating the bill

and applying the factor…

the English factor

of multiplication.

"A lovely old place, monsieur,

but the walls are all damp,

the timbers, mon Dieu,

have you ever seen worms this big?"

But the food is so fresh

in the supermarket trolley,

and the air so clean,

and that view,

romantic, beautiful...

It's all so... French!

"We can start the work

next Tuesday week, monsieur...

probably".

MISS YOU

The day job, the one that paid for the renovation of the Devon farmhouse, often took me away for days at a time. This is a reflection on those distant days and how I felt being away from Karen.

There was a time known as "Before",

when there were people known as "Others",

a time of high words and overblown gestures,

of dissatisfactions borne of the deepest well,

a time of searching in the blind of snow white storms.

"I was lost but now am found",

so say words in heavily bound history,

stories upon which some profess their faith.

But I have closed the book

on those old and dusty chapters.

I have filled that open wound-spring

with the loose stones and powder drifts

of discontent and misplaced hopes.

With you or without you,

separated by a skin's thickness

or separated by days and miles,

there is one place and one time,

there is no before and no other.

There is simply this; that I love you

and that I miss you to my core

when we are apart.

OUT OF THE WALLED GARDEN

As a counterpoint to Into The Walled Garden, this is a reflection one a more hopeful view of the world, where difficulties are overcome and we can flourish even if late in the day.

We start with the careful plantsman

corralling ox-eye daisies into square patches of earth,

neatly boxed next to upright beds of nicotiana.

In the scheme of things, in the planning

and right-angled digging of things,

he would shave the grass, blade by blade,

and fix the shape of nature to his eye.

Fence panels were always creosote brown

and absolutely perpendicular to paving slabs.

Even birds were commanded to be quiet.

The bow of rose pink blooms

that crowned the thorn in his side

would nod not to the sun but to his frown.

Strange then the blooming of forget-me-nots

in the now autumn sun.

The hands on his pocket watch

have ceased to turn with the hours,

and so the riot of creeper and running root

has spread chaos in the borders of his garden.

Colours mix and merge in these late days,

gabbling through grainy showers,

chattering along with the chirrup of birdsong.

The ox-eye daisies join

with the free-flowing discourse,

but keep one eye firmly

on the shadows at their shoulder,

happy in different days

but some whiles sad now that times

have changed for the better.

THE COLOUR OF HER EYES

Rooted in a memory from my university days, this was triggered by a particularly vivid dream. There's something here about the impossibility of knowing someone. I think that there may also be a hint here about my fascination with folklore and fairy tales.

Sealed in square cut ice

and borne on a plinth of rough wood,

shaped without hand or saw or plane,

lies the most beautiful woman in the world.

She dreams in a timeless land of cold days,

fallen in an avalanche of snow,

sleeping like Beauty awaiting her prince

these thousand years.

A cameo of perfection,

she exists in burning mists,

as does the image of a lover

on the closed eyelid of a young man,

who drifts off to night dark

with a smile on his hidden, solitary face.

She is as fresh as an early morning

and as bright as the unfolding yellow brilliance

of evening primrose at the end of a warm summer day.

You have to remember to breathe in her presence.

The great hands of Florence and Rome

have fashioned her face in stone and marble.

The flashing minds and eyes that conjure celluloid images

have made her face stand a thousand hands high

in dark halls a world over, flooding space

with the milk of her bones and the moon of her flesh,

freezing the blood of boys in the winged shell of her smile

and the iridescence of her eyes.

The carved, melded space in the ice

is devoutly quiet, is free of shape and image,

a suggestion of all that she is and nothing more.

Stood here before her on bare floor timbers,

I ask myself questions;

"What colour is her hair?"

"How tall is she?"

Set free from the ice

the answers to these questions

might fly the warm breeze,

wrapping themselves

around the moth candle flame

in wisps of smoke that echo centuries

and seconds of flow and time.

"Would her hair be blonde-white

or thick and finger curled brunette?"

The answer is unimportant.

She lies in ice,

without form,

unseeing and unseen,

except that there is this...

If by some far miracle

she should open her eyelids

within the sapphire of this giant's rings

and look at me,

I know what colour her eyes would be.

And as it is this that I know,

I know also that she calls me,

that she makes me lay my hand

on the ice tomb that encases her shape

and that I will gladly fly

like a moth into the flame

to be consumed by her.

SCREAMING AT THE SEA

This piece came about during a short break one February in Cornwall. A relationship that I was in at the time was on the wane and I felt safe shouting out some frustrations into a howling onshore gale, safe in the knowledge that no one else was on the beach to hear me.

Standing below slipping walls of rock,

carved and sheared by ages, salt whipped,

weathered by sharp blade winds,

slabs, the size of cars,

tumble upon sand and stone.

I clambered over them,

hands and sand encrusted boots

slipping on their liquid skins,

cold fingers, wrinkling at the tips,

grown numb beneath a blown grey sky.

Below my scramble I saw e a cave,

dark, damp, with rippling rift pools at its entrance.

Jumping, sliding on sandstone,

I stood under its overhanging, trembling lip

and watched the ragged edges

of a blue plastic milk crate sway gently

amid swollen branches and summer derelicts.

Looking up, swallowed by the flooding curtain wall,

smothered by oozing shadows under a dun sky

I felt giddy with sheer scale and racing clouds.

Staring out at a wild and dissonant sea,

merging, mongrel woven into unrefined sky,

the space between us rolled, inbound,

curled on wings of surf topped swell.

My boots were thick and heavy with clinging sand

as I stepped out across the puckered tidal plain,

my coat squalling around my sinking legs,

hair blowing across my forehead,

pushing on through the lifting spray,

streaming, out to the edge of the world.

Screaming at the sea,

amplifying, eyes gouged deep and wide,

hurting the back of my throat.

Deep draughts exhaled violently,

arms spread wide, forcing, expelling the word.

Resurrection comes with nails...

and with the Demons out upon the wind,

humouring the surf,

I walked back towards higher ground,

limp, sticky with salt spray wind

and quieter with the world.

HIGHFORD WINTER

I wrote a series of seasonal pieces while working to restore Highford Farm during the early 2000s, an attempt to capture the essence of the place as we moved through the year. The farm is located atop a Devon hill near Clovelly, facing squarely onto the Atlantic.

Winter run-off gabbles down twig litter gullets

that edge rain sodden fields, banked high,

pushing upwards from an unbreaking sea,

white curl painted on grey-blue horizons.

Blackthorn spikes stand to in the wind,

snagging blue liners and ragged feed bags

that sound like sails running loose before the wind.

In a corner, down by the owl-tree,

machine skeletons rust in the shaved ground,

and written on a stone in black marker,

the words; "Misty, forever in our hearts",

are garnished by a bracken slimed jam jar

The stream fusses on through twisted roots

nibbling at the soft walled banks, felling decayed bark,

and tree limbs, heavy with lichens, droop to windward,

while emaciated Docks, thick and matted,

whisper through horizontal sheets of rain

that cover the paths that lead to the grey wall sea,

a rain unending, sheeting down

to the breaking cliff falls.

SEVEN OF EIGHT

I cannot remember where I read about the physics behind the visible tracer bullet, but I do remember stories early in my adult life about British troops in what was then Aden watching tracer lines criss-cross the night sky above Crater. There's obviously some sort of fascination here for me in this subject, this piece stemming from a description in Buchheim's Das Boot.

Here, upon the water,

I drift on a tide of eyes that saw the tracer.

One of eight was silent,

its report an orphan child leading the pack.

Two of eight was sound,

the action bell rising out of bland routine.

Three of eight was shock,

a spur of blood in arteries and shredded veins.

Four of eight was fear,

an involuntary step towards the sound of bedlam.

Five of eight was action,

unthinking, unwinding, the process of fighting back.

Six of eight was wonder,

exhilaration, real life spinning on rifled adrenalin .

Seven of eight was mortal,

the scything of stems, cutting down the flower of life.

Eight of eight was a dark doorway,

a pulse of fire receding into a night black swell.

(You only ever see the seventh bullet in a line of tracers - a trick of light and optical awareness)

WORDS FAIL ME

A simple moment – that first waking on a quiet day, where the love of your life is soft and gentle and rising to greet the day through her own cobwebbed sleep.

Words fail me in the lightness of the morning,

where cobwebs hang with dew in the corners of windows,

caught in the softly peeling wind

that pulls sleeping heads from shallow breath.

Warm in the heart of rain that streaks the glass,

dry in the melt of waking, I can curl sounds,

but rarely is there any sense of my thoughts

in the mess of syllable and teacup clutter.

You ask me why it is that words fail me

in the lightness of the morning, where cobwebs

hang with dew in the corners of windows?

There is no other way, no other sense to being,

but to be with you. Feeling the tremors of your life

merge with mine through every play of day

and every shade of night is the whole.

I catch my breath, dazzled by your reflection

in the diamond mask of soft spun thread

that drips sunlight on the morning air,

and cannot speak a single word, my love.

It is, then, in the darkling cast of evening,

when the fox barks and the owls extend white fingers,

that words come with the scratch of the pen.

BLESSED BY THE MOON'S BLUSH

This is a nightmare sequence taken from a repeating dream. I've always dreamed vividly and a number of those dreams, or at least their obvious themes repeat often. From memory this was a dream that came to me on the farm in Devon when Karen was battling cancer.

Outward Bound...

She is longshore speed,

a full press of sail on the stairs,

a creature of the eager, half trodden

floorboard world where door bolts grumble,

catching at streaming dressing gown chords,

and the quiet of the night snuffs out

the candle glow of safely lit days.

Her shadowed fingers hold wood

and swing open a door, through which

midnight-sweet flowers scent

the high arc of sky that bends away

and down towards the edge of the world,

where surf curls and spray whips

at matelot faces as they tumble down

and over the final, endless precipice.

With their disconsolate roar

fading in her ringing ears,

and left high, dry and alone,

leaves ripple softly around her.

The silence of the world is bare

on her skin, witnessed by dreaming birds,

snuffling hedgerow rooters

and the unseen undergrowth scuffle.

The grass under her feet is dewy,

as warmly moist as she imagines

a tongue might be on her breast

and the air is a miracle of peace.

Becalmed…

She is like the Old Man of the Sea,

dawdling her way through the dewy swell,

letting the hidden objects of the garden,

a domestic tide of flotsam and jetsam,

branches, wilting flower heads,

the rose of an old metal watering can

and the arms of an old wooden bench,

brush against her thinly veiled cotton legs.

She swims in a water of space and time,

through darkly solid currents

where shadow things spill into her veins

like black, spiced rum.

Above her head, carousing with the falling waves,

clouds roll off across roof tops,

grey-white banks reflecting moonbeams,

diving, disappearing and emerging again

in strange headed animal shapes

before they lose themselves

in the distance between her hair

and the stars.

Running before the Storm...

The sky is too big

and she too young to hold on to it,

too alone in the vast ocean world.

Panic, that alien wave of terror,

the losing of herself,

crashes in from the growling cloudscape,

and drunk on the velvet draught,

defenceless in the path of the running sea,

she spins and runs,

stumbling over blades of razor grass,

menaced by torn branches

and the predatory grin of circling,

shark-finned garden furniture.

Her hair catches in will-o'-the-wisp claws,

and reeling, dodging to the left, skipping,

falling away from the rose heads,

she hears behind her, close,

the tearing sound made by ripping cloth.

With blood on the soles of her feet,

with her eyes tightly shut,

hard knuckled and white,

she slams the door shut, pants,

gulps down air and curls herself

up into a hedgehog ball

at the foot of the stairs.

EVIDENCE OF SLEEP

As a counterpoint to the last piece, this poem attempts to catch the mundanity of waking mid-way through the night. In particular this come from our sojourn in Caerwent, when Karen was in remission and life appeared to be reverting to some sort of normality.

It's dark in the waking,

the soul sound is breathing,

your own, and you turn to look

at the digital enlightenment

of a radio-alarm, small hours,

the evidence of sleep,

turning, restlessly squirming

in the luxury of yesterday's

new sheets and duvet cover,

and you yawn.

The bed creaks,

you hold still, vague,

still night-dreaming,

and you hear faint strains of music,

a tin sound, distant, a radio,

wind in the telephone wires,

a television, blue and soft

milk float automation,

the country alive at night,

downtime city life,

melodic repetition,

the guts of the piece,

violin, guitar, obscure chords

leaping and diving, dancing

on singing wires,

dribbling into the pillow.

A dog barks...and another.

A car passes by your window.

Burying yourself in the soft down,

you sink away, forgetting

the signs and certainties

of a briefly remembered dream.

OUR LADY OF SILENCE

Another of the cancer pieces – this one centred on my sense of loss even though Karen was still very much alive at the time. There was a constant battle between the day-time positivity needed to be a part of the solution and the dark hours of doubt and guilt..

He is a shadow breathing,

a mass darker on the still air,

thin, smouldering and black,

hands trembling, adrenalin spiked,

imagining the moment

when he pulls the sheet

from her body, when he begins

to peel back her skin

so that he can expose her essence,

her true beauty,

through layers of muscle,

bone and soft tissue.

He is a shadow breathing hard,

A thing of definite substance,

sharp and wide-eyed

as he pulls back the first

soft white cotton sheet,

revealing another beneath it.

He pulls this sheet off her body,

anticipating the climax, her nakedness,

and pulls and pulls again,

sheet after sheet after twisting sheet,

until her contours disintegrate,

and reveal an empty bed.

The indent where someone has lain,

the depressions and gullies,

are still warm with body heat.

WHY THE DOG GOES EARLY TO BED...

I worked away from home for many years, usually leaving on a Sunday night or very early on a Monday, returning home late on a Friday night. One of the joys of the week was opening the front door, shrugging off the week and snuggling down with Karen & Jonesy, our rescue hound, especially in winter when the fire was set and the Aga was warming the farm kitchen.

This Corbières tastes red,

thick and full of firelight fruit,

like smoke on my tongue.

I sit on the floor

and lean back into her arms.

She moves forward,

blue eyes, reflections,

flames and sun fire embers.

We touch lips, grazing skin,

lost in a fugue of sound

and the soft descent of amber nights.

We taste flesh,

imprinting our shape,

into soft crimson cushions.

Her hair, shoulder length,

is a cascade of fine sea mist

falling across my face.

Eyes close in ruby shadows.

I feel her weight, a whisper,

urgent to be loved.

COLD SHORE BALLAD

In the Fireside Tales collections I have taken a lifelong fascination with folklore and fairy tales and turned that interest into a grand project. This is an early piece that reflects that interest, an attempt to tell a story. I remember listening to a lot of Sinead O'Connor at the time and I can hear her influence in this as well.

I am the wind, the voice of the gale-howl,

the shriek in a sleepless night,

the sigh that softens stone and heart,

I am the seal head on grey surge surf,

the white bobbing gull maiden,

the breath of a woman waiting

these long-drawn years for the footstep,

for the glad home rising swell of hobnails

and the drag of a sledge on cobbles,

I am the fishwife knifing the raw knuckle catch,

waiting, squall watching, break-sea casting,

my eyes curled over horizons, foam flecked,

watching out for my boy, my man, my own.

On a tide swell moon, a vengeful night,

the sea towered, Babylon a-rearing,

riding the black backs of hag-hounds,

and with lanterns bob-bobbing

along the headland cliffs,

an oilskinned daisy chain formed.

The sound of rocks and shingle falling,

sliding, crashing, splintering,

made us hunker down, squatting,

terrorised in the shawl-shiver,

made us hear the crust buckle 'neath out feet.

They came then and laid bare the bones

of his drowning, sure in the fact

that no man, no sainted wood,

no living thing could stand such an ocean,

such a spite, such a warmongering

amongst the waves and deeps and storm laced airs,

I told 'em, spat in their salt smart eyes,

I cried clear to Him in His sunlit glories

that my man could never be lost,

not as long as a heart beat within me.

Cursed they said I was for the words I used,

and cursed I was by them as spoke so rude.

Touched, a speak-no-more they called me,

a lost maid, a watcher amongst the fish corpses.

But I know these shores, as did he, the tides,

the banks, the beds, the shallows and the deeps,

the shift and shelter even in the chasm seas,

and he'll be back, I said, back in the days of sun,

back in the winter rains and the chill nights,

warming me by the fire with his touch,

with his breath hot on my face,

with his tales and tally and salt calluses.

He'll be back, I cried to the scour-winds,

to drag the boats up onto the shingles

in the lean months, picking at nets

and shuttling his lines, to scrimp

and scavenge, to scrape clean,

making good and making me belly fat

with his shape and his sinew.

I cried then upon the star cold shore,

as I cry now upon these cloud cold winds,

calling his name, his face withering in my mind,

as I withered of skin and strength,

the spent days of my age and infirmity gaoled,

cast into mirrors of loneliness,

into the image of him as he was, as I was.

But things lessen, reduce, fade away,

fading we two into the grey sea water,

into the crawling mist that rolls over the land,

the damp air pulling me down to the cold stone

of the headland and the headstone

by a forgotten grave, his name obscured,

but written still in these brown earth bones

that found no rest in life and stir still

in the cradle, in the endless waiting.

I am the seal head on black water,

the gull maid, the sea mist,

the sigh on the point, the squall wraith.

My eyes are the gleam of sunlight

on rock surf spray, my path the way of

the setting sun on the calm blue-black

of a summer eve.

Aye, I am the wind,

I am the voice of the gale-howl,

the shriek in the sleepless night,

the sigh that softens stone and heart.

I am the seal head on grey surf,

the white bobbing gull maiden,

the breath of a woman waiting

these long drawn years for the footstep,

I am the ghost, the watcher in the deep

these two hundred years and more.

So listen well, you sons of men,

to the suck and the draw,

hear me on the shallow breeze,

come sit with me on cliff tops in my howling,

listen to me riding old Babylon's coat tails,

feel my tears in the rain that falls and see me,

the watching grey head off the quay,

waiting for his homeward bound sail,

unfurled and full, off this star cold shore.

FOR THE LONG DOWN ROAD

Truth be told I've always liked a drink. There's a family thing here, given that I share genes on both sides with some serious imbibers or old. Family stories. This piece comes from a period where time and tide and circumstance made me stop and think about my own relationship with the demon drink.

It comes like hallelujah, an evangelical chorus,

a beating of breasts in the red light of deep nights,

a commitment, the full bore, whole-hog embrace,

a snaking line of party hats and staccato elbows,

the speaking in tongues that comes by degree

rather than absolute shocking blue revelation.

It is the host, the revel, arms locked in arms,

the break of dance and palsied eye, the sleepless lids

and sallow skin that bids farewell poor innocence,

a learning of rules and words in cups, draughted

and drawn, the drinking down of the long road

that winds it's easy path along the ways of lost days.

This is a serious dedication to alcohol in low light places,

chosen because your smile can't be seen

among so many lunatic grins,

where you become faceless among the beloved,

and so, in the company of those

who gutter in the wind like you do,

you slowly wind on the clock, tripping dully

through the sag of years until you run out of geography.

JOHN, TERRORIST

John did quite well for me in competition and anthology. For the life of me I cannot remember the precise origins of this piece, other than a general sense of protest and impotence.

If I could sing,

I'd bum Beach Boy notes at bar-bar bar-bar bar mitzvahs,

If I could cook,

I'd revolutionise fast food, burning prayer wheels on the barbie for the Buddha.

If I could act,

I'd be the son of a preacher man, smouldering darkly for the girls.

If I could answer questions,

I'd ask the Elephant God what happened to the Elephant Man.

If I could write,

I'd leave a note cancelling the eggs for the milkman on my way up
to heaven.

If I could play the piano,

I'd tinkle the flight of the Bumble Bee for passengers as we hit the
skyscraper.

I can do none of these things;

and so I'm less than the whole,

an unfinished product in this celebrated world,

I'm John, Gainsayer, Dragon Slayer.

I'm evenly balanced, the chips on both shoulders

delicately poised, even though they prevent me

from leaving the bar where I hold court

on fat slags and bloody arseholes.

This is my stage, where you'll hear of the labours

of John, Terrorist, moving inexorably, inevitably,

closer to heaven with a hole in his shoe.

PRINCESS OF THE WESTERN WORLD

One of the girls, no names nor pack drills, had a wee bit of a moment when she received the wrong version of a well-known dress-up doll. Made me think about the whole process around gift giving and the expectations that we all have...

I don't want it, I don't want it, I don't want it,

not that one, it's boring, look at it,

I don't want a working Barbie,

who wants a working Barbie,

it's just not fair, it's so boring,

look at the clothes, what is it again,

Air Hostess Barbie, that's so horrid,

where's her pretty blue ribbons,

where's her lace, her fairy dress,

look at those shoes, brown, yuck,

where are her glass slippers,

where's the smile, her happy face,

she looks like she's frowning,

and her hair, it's so mousy and dull,

like her shoes,

I want my very own Goldilocks,

I want one just like Lady Di,

in sequins and tiaras,

the world at her dainty emerald feet,

I hate it, I hate it, I hate it,

the box isn't very pretty,

and it's so small, so tiny,

you can't make a fairy castle

out of something like that,

I don't want this one, it's not fair,

I hate it, I want one like me.

THE MAN WITH THE SNAKE OIL TONGUE

Having read Something Wicked This Way Comes by Ray Bradbury, I rather fell in love with the image of the carnie huckster, the carpetbagger, the bunko man. This is firmly based in the ideas and the images from Bradbury's story and I make no apologies for that. The scene touched me deeply. I may also have been listening to Orbital's Snivilisation album quite a lot – I Wish I Had Duck Feet…

"Roll up, roll up and see the show, ladies and gentlemen,

be amazed, be stunned, prepare to witness the wonders of the age,

right here, right now.

The realm of the phantasm awaits your incredulous eyes,

beguiling, intriguing and just a little frightening,

but worry not, my dears, my beloveds, for this is the end of the pier

and not the end of the world".

Breathless with running free from school,

hot with excitement, a cold copper in my hot pocket hand,

I watched the man whose eyes danced

in the torch song sway of red and white carnival stripes,

as he called us in, one by one, with a smile as wide as an ocean,

a carnivore smile, waiting for life to crawl out of the surf

and onto the palate of dry land.

"Roll up, roll up and see the show,

be astounded by the bearded lady,

every inch of her body alive with fur,

witness the incredible rubber man,

who's limbs will tie themselves in knots,

see the two-headed talking calf

in fatted conversation with himself,

oh yes, oh my, we have it all,

walk on up and feel the thrill of danger,

experience the cold edge of delight course in your veins,

feel the heat of fired earth running down your spines".

Hypnotised by traces of lantern smoke on still air,

lost in the trance of his lilting voice and fantastic wit,

I swear he caught me with a long cool glance.

His eyes danced, measuring me for size and weight,

and with that look my eager legs pulled me forward,

stepping lightly into the darkness within,

into the heat of bodies under canvas,

waiting, expecting, shivering through electric dreams

and 'Hey Presto' clouds.

"Roll up, roll up, room for one more,

Yes, you, Madam, come inside

and find the meaning of life revealed,

be dumbfounded by the Sumatran Ape Boy,

who can peel soft fruits with his incredible hand-like toes,

see the amazing calculating device that directs

financial markets across our green hilled globe,

be astonished by the fantastical plastic box of pictures,

pictures, my friends, drawn upon thin air,

observe the humble bean, yes, I said bean,

that can be any food or drink that you care to imagine,

be brave, be foolish, be anything you want to be,

ladies and gentlemen, no one will see you in here".

He stood on a platform off to our right, naked to the waist,

his skin rippling with muscle, oiled and tanned,

his hair, falling from under a high felt hat onto his shoulders, an impious gleam in eyes,

eyes that seemed to move of their own free will.

His hands rose up to the full height of the tent,

touching the ribbed sheets of canvas

as he expelled air from his lungs

in loud bursts of hyperbole,

sending waves of searing heat into the crowd,

chilling the sweat on our faces.

"Behold the wonderful horseless carriage

driven by a headless coachman dressed in crepe,

feel the heady intoxication of the flower seed

that a million addicts ingest on the back of a spoon,

hear the thunder of rapid-fire projectiles

as they sweep away the blossom of a generation,

gasp in awe at the incredible vanishing woman,

who will vanish right before your very eyes,

never to be seen again,

read with shock and disbelief

the document that launched a thousand gunships,

with never a true word upon any one of its pages,

see the world's strongest man lift an acorn

without breaking into a sweat,

my dears, my darlings, all these I give to you and more,

so much more!"

As his last syllable lifted, balloon like, on hot air

and the tent flaps squirmed away from us,

he turned to me, as he seemed to turn to everyone else,

appearing as if from nowhere at our sides

and clapping us on the shoulders.

He tilted his head to the left and grinned,

gap toothed charming

while the astonishing cavalcade played again

in our dazzled eyes.

"Give me another penny, boy", he said,

"and I'll give you the world,

I'll let you meet the ape boy;

you can drive with the headless coachman,

you can breathe the smoke of the flower drug".

I couldn't answer at first.

His scent, the scent of straw bedded animals,

filled my head, and he waited, nodding,

knowing the shape of my thoughts.

"I have no more money", I whispered,

and he laughed the crowds away

like an owl hunting on dusk down,

so that only he and I remained in the world,

clothed in midnight's rich, thick oils,

his sweet eyes locked on mine.

He sang a velvet lullaby as we walked,

my cheek pressed firmly into the rippling skin

and muscle of his ribs;

"Forget the penny, lad, you can owe me."

BOY COMES HOME

I out this together while in America during the early stages of the Iraq conflict after 9/11. It is probably a little naïve but watching television footage in a hotel room in Miami made me feel distinctly uneasy with the world and my own participation in day-to-day events that could never touch on the reality experienced by so many men and women, most of them very much younger than me.

Superpower blades, hot metal chirruping,

cases streaming, metal jacket rhythms,

dust in his eyes despite the goggles,

sand in his boots, sweating, hot air on dry skin,

grit in his swollen throat, obscured vision,

Hummer-hummings, burning rubber,

concrete ripped, twisted reinforcing rods laid bare,

orders, rags, boys and guns, mixed together,

spiced and sliced, dominating, shock and awe,

a Superpower on the move, targeted, logical,

overwhelming, lethal, high on an explosive charge,

fear and loathing, a film score playing in their heads,

a world full of thunder flashes, Coke tins litter the gutter,

and the boy, one confused soul running scared

with the rest of the howling pack,

dodges bullet tracers...Hollywood calling.

The boy feels the shock and awe of jagged metal

and fighting for breath sees blood in the dirt.

He tries to make sense of the place and the faces

a picture forms, home, his mother's face, an imprint,

a boot in the sand, slow recognition, a GI's boot,

regular issue.

Then the shouting, the screaming and groaning,

mechanised, MEDIC, MEDIC, for fucks sake, MEDIC!

Sounds fade and dissolve into the hum of engines,

he feels hands, is aware but absent with leave,

and drifts away from the chop of automatic light arms

under the cover of Superpower blades.

BUTTERFLY

September 2005. Karen and I married at High Bullen, North Devon, the entire party staying at the house or at local pubs. It was a bright, sunny and warm day, the light sparkling with excitement. I wrote this for Karen.

You don't think that I hear one single word you say,

that your words flutter in and out of focus

like the wings of a butterfly caught in the light

reflecting off of early morning dew laced leaves

and drooping flower heads that wait to kiss the sun.

You think that I am bound in some theory of chaos,

wrapped in feathers that spin up into bright skies

on winds that sweep across peninsular headlands,

bending trees to the East and to the South.

It is true, true that I spin, that I turn somersaults

on summer breezes and that I rattle my cage bars

with the breaking tips of my wings,

but it is only true because you speak to me,

because you hold me, because you wrap me in spells

and wells of deep drawn airs.

It is only true because

I am drenched in your cool shadows

under these wind bent branches.

I hear every word that you say,

and I skittle the lanes with nothing other

than the dream of your words' shape,

of their richness, of their boldness,

and so, on the wing, swallow tailing,

I spend these summer, these autumn hours

in the bright sunlight of happiness and contentment,

dressed in your loving and in your knowing of love.

HAVERSHAM

Sometimes, after fifteen years or so of neglect, it's not always clear what the motivation behind each piece really was. I do remember elements of this being a reflection on the blear-eyed small hours limp to the toilet after a few too many, as imagined when you hear the inevitable bumping into things as you too wake up.

The cat's mother prowls the house at night

wearing that eternal seductress frock;

Terry towelling, a dressing gown, and slippers...

she's drunk too much Shiraz,

and muzzy with dehydration,

confused in the kindling hours,

has woken, desperate for the lav,

dissipated, walking the landing,

dark, silent, wrapped and soundless,

absorbed in the absent slough of skin on skin,

she shivers at the creak of a floorboard,

the signature of her solitude, alone,

without time and keepsakes,

and she wants to stop the clock,

fuck, fuck, fuck... a poetic image,

at Hugh Grant's funeral in a mini skirt...

So she opens the clock's face plate

and placing her left-hand index finger

upon the hour hand,

she believes that she can stop

the passing of days, and that she,

being some vague mistress Haversham

in her wedding dress ways,

oblivious to the stains that she absorbs

through the lining of the hem

of her bright, brittle, night gown,

can rearrange the furniture

of her long train fate.

A SHORT HISTORY OF OLD BUILDINGS

A little like Closing Of The Chapel, this poem was borne out of moments wandering and waiting in London streets. A lot of that time was spent collecting take-away meals while working away from home, usually hanging around outside the shop to smoke a cigarette. I used to let my thoughts meander on the architecture and the history of the buildings I saw as I walked those suburban streets.

In the graveyard street where carrier bags go to die,

snagging around the roots of peeling plane trees,

houses sit quietly, queuing for the knacker's yard,

down at heel in flaking, exhaust leeched brickwork,

hand-me-downs, plodding ever so softly southwards

towards the valley bottom.

Behind unhooked curtains,

dull rooms peel paint and spot with black spore damp

where the plaster still adheres to exposed rib lathes.

The sky is winter pale with a light, chill breeze

cutting through rotten window frames

that hang on grimly to a wall above a pillared porch,

the stone of which is chipped and cracked,

the cornices gone to dust.

This was architecture.

Another branch of the human race

lived here once upon a time,

when inner city suburban had yet to metamorphose

into bleached wood shabbiness.

Doors were painted gloss red

and the hollowed doorsteps

were scrubbed daily.

These were solid homes,

stately in a small, urban way,

firm and secure in a little money

and a brief spell of leisure.

The parlours were full of music

and drifting fire smoke,

full of chatter and conversation,

lit by burnished brass candlesticks,

and scented by roasting meat

and thick black coal.

The satisfaction in these streets

has twisted and crumbled,

has become overburdened with humanity.

Gardens reek with waste

and last year's rotting, overgrown grass heads.

These houses are offerings to ruin

in their luxurious pensions,

offerings left to the crows

and to the wide-open winter skies

seen from behind tatty grey nets

and holes in broken roofs.

Behind one of the scuff-fronted doors a baby cries out,

a caterwaul summoning of lost opportunities,

a call to a God who obviously has better things to do

on a sapping January afternoon

than listen to prayers.

CANCER WARD

The title makes the root of this piece rather obvious, being one of a series related to Karen's illness and my download and processing of living grief. Watching some being sliced away, day by slow day, drains your strength – the one thing that you need to maintain in order to be at all effective in supporting the person going through their own Hell on earth.

The bar is open, and although

I know better than this,

am more than intelligent enough

to understand the consequences,

I find myself joining the rest

of the lonely drunks sitting in dusty,

dimly lit corners nursing medication

at a table still showing glass rings

and awash with slops

from the last unsteady hand.

Here I am believing

that I don't need anyone

or anything to help me deal

with visits to the cancer ward.

It's one way to handle things,

this forgetting,

but the doors revolve,

spinning us in and out

of each other's company,

when all I really want is to lay down,

is to have her lay down with me

when it gets dark so that together

we can forget about the world

for a quiet moment or two.

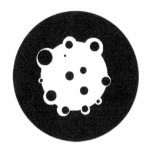

DIRTY TUMOURS

No getting away from the cancer series, I'm afraid. Four years of fighting, hoping, re-setting and going again makes for a fair few nights alone in the study while your partner deals with the aftermath of chemotherapy or some such treatment. Too much time to reflect, possibly...

The abnormal replication of cells is

a subject made clear by Chinese whispers.

My darling girl drags herself from her poison bed,

puts on her new head, and smiles.

The word metastasise describes the movement

of a spinning top as gravity and friction pull it down.

I brandish my loyalty like a placard waving anti-nuke,

exorcising the ghosts of the future, bell, book and candle.

At my core, I am an ambiguous thing,

spinning through vague compass points.

My darling girl paints eyebrows onto a blank canvas,

and we swap freak wigs at parties.

In the night my right hand cups her left breast,

my forearm on the scar running across her chest,

When she wakes in the morning and I watch her dress,

she fits her new shapes together and I smile.

She smiles back at me and insanity bubbles up.

I remember the words we exchanged about love.

Tomorrow the cycle will repeat itself.

Tomorrow I will be braver.

EXPLORER 242

We liked to ramble with the dog, Jonesy. Hardly an original pastime, and mapping life's journey onto the symbols on a map is hardly original either. All of that said, I have always had a soft spot for this piece, which made it into a couple of anthologies as well, so maybe not quite as bad as all that.

dual carriageway

  place of worship with tower

    ground survey site

     the map inside

       folded, creased, torn

       missing data, incomplete

     standard gauge,

   landfill site or slag heap

site of battle

the view from this hill

  has variable points of reference

    sometimes I get lost.

    Normal tidal limit

      other road or track

      public convenience

    taking time, making false turns

    and unexpected discoveries

    walking without a destination

    triangulation pillar

  bracken, heath or rough grassland

permitted footpath.

QUIET TIME IN A CROWD

Working away from home for sustained periods means that you get a lot of time to yourself. Hotel rooms and temporary apartment rentals can be pretty soulless (although good for uninterrupted writing time). This piece originated in an early summer evening in London when I took a moment walking through a garden square near Covent Garden to contemplate being alone in a crowd.

Surrounded by knees and shopping bags,

by the sound of feet and the trilling of mobile phones,

swamped by shoe leather and calf skin briefcases

following a trail of Costa-packet coffee cups,

and the flapping skins of discarded sandwiches,

fighting for aqualung breath on city streets,

she sits on the grass, in full and broad noon sun,

counting the tireless legs of worker bees

as they bumble between flowers

bunched in municipally maintained beds and banks of colour.

The pavements shimmer heat haze,

Phrasing words within the rumble of wheels and blades.

The world around her, viewed at the level of writing

on skipping plastic carrier bags,

is a ring-a-ring-o'-roses dance

of dusty souvenirs and lunch hour errands,

bursting with possibilities and goodies from

factory gates, a world full to brimming

with superannuated school kids toting their satchels

from gate to lesson and home again,

and all done to the high descant beat of playground songs.

She can feel the unexpected hardness of grass

imprinting on the backs of her legs.

She can smell earth on her fingers as she leans back

with her face open to ultra-violet light,

and she shuts her eyes, letting the red-hot burn of combustion

and the sounds of the crowd wash over her

before she too has to grumble her way back

to the counting of pollen.

LITTLE BLACK RAIN CLOUD

A dream sequence, no doubt influenced by something I was reading at the time. I forget the actual inspiration. Sometime after this was written, and long after I'd left this buried in a folder, I remember listening to Peter Murphy's The Prince and Old Lady Shade. I had to dig this out once more, so here you are...

La Belle Madame hangs half way

between heaven and earth,

Mary Poppins in mourning crepes,

sucking at a crow veil of black lace

that falls darkly over her face,

layering deep, bruised shadows

where her cheek bones should be,

while her skeletal, bat claw hands

clutch at the ringlet edge of a cloud,

and her legs kick at the mocking air,

thrashing at raindrops to shake them loose,

free to pour down on our heads

as we stumble, keen and avid,

between carnival tents and gaudy caravans,

our shoes and trouser legs covered

in muddy splashes.

La Belle Madame drifts on trade winds,

spitting thunder at the roof of the world,

dragging her harlequinade, her circus

of ring-a-rosy booths and rusty cages

across oceans and long back roads,

so that each and every one of us can gaze,

wide eyed and slack jawed,

at the incredible bearded lady,

who seems, on her second coming,

when the years have passed through us,

to be something less than she was,

to be a caricature of the unorthodox glory

we remember from our personal history.

La Belle Madame, driven on to windward

by the gulf stream, knuckle-white

and rag-feathered, as thin as a stick woman,

a bag of bones beneath her crepes

and billowing black satin petticoats,

hangs half way to heaven

because that's as far as she'll ever get,

that's the price that she pays

for charging a clipped penny a peek

at the freaks in the greatest show

that's ever been seen down here

on the wet, wet earth spinning

beneath her wildly bicycling feet.

ON THE DOORSTEP

When I still enjoyed a cigarette or cigar, and when it became less and less socially acceptable to smoke in the house, I, like so many of us, found myself spending hours standing on the doorstep late at night listening to the world. I rarely ever think of such things now, but when I do I remember those moments fondly. Not that there's anything stopping me from just standing on the doorstep...

In the ghost night, when the wind blows

you need to shield the match with your hand

to keep the flame alive and to smoke

under a starless sky.

The spark catches on background sounds

of footsteps and car doors slamming,

under distant shouts and owl hoots,

and dogs sniffing at the edges of the park.

Kids run free after bedtime,

dropping glass and polystyrene,

the shadow country appearing limitless

with immoderate opportunity,

and at the charnel time,

when the rest of the ghosts come out to smoke,

I remember the sleep of other souls through time,

cheating, sneaking another breath, another moment,

and we all flicker, choreographed, striking matches,

flaming briefly in the vastness of space.

PRETTY IN PINK

Pretty In Pink is a requested piece that I am very fond of as I wrote it for my step-daughter, Emma and her husband, Doug, on the occasion of their wedding. It was a grand day at a lovely barn near Cirencester, where Karen and I were living having given up the Devon farm to be closer to family while Karen battled her illness.

Dusted in summer flushed silks

and bright white cottons,

in party frocks and glad rags,

nervous and strangely silent,

biting their lips and thrown

on their beam ends,

a girl and a boy remind us

of the days that have passed

since they were five years old,

dressed now in the same skin

and colours as they were

when they played infectious smiles

and screaming games

in distant August heat waves.

Their shapes are grown,

their features more clearly defined,

they are styled, but they are still,

if only in the mind, in snapshots,

someone's little darlings.

The summer toys that lay

scattered on dry grass

have been cleared away,

and the endless questions

of the breathless five year old

have passed through

the blossoming certainties

of double digit thresholds

and crashed into the sheer

bloody-minded torments

of scrambling teenage uncertainty.

Hopes for upland futures,

have changed as quickly

as rolling cloud banks.

The trials of parental love

have built tender friendships,

and evolved into this bright day,

so full of the rich, sweet

and maturing birdsong

of young adult lives.

Wrapped in histories of

dusty pinks, abrasive attitudes

and the hang dog lazy

lethargy of late nights,

a little girl and a little boy

wait nervously to leave this place

of velvet heat and soft shadow,

pretty in pink and all grown up.

SHORT-SIGHTED BEES

I read something in, I think, The New Scientist that sparked this gentle little piece off. As a keen but very amateur gardener, and with the threats facing pollinators, this seemed like a small way of praying for better times while acknowledging the pettiness of our personal gripes.

Mornings break differently now that summer is here,

although in my dowdy shuffle towards ever shorter days

the urgency that once shovelled itself upon my waking

is now a spent force. The slowing of the physical is at odds

with the apparent speeding up of time, but on a sunny afternoon,

when bees and hover flies make a virtue of work,

I have discovered delight in lifting petulance and annoyance

from the simple beauty that shines

when these hurried little creatures

mistake me, in my withered state, for a flower.

THE INSOMNIAC BOOTH

There is a paragraph in one of James Lee Burke's novels where the main protagonist, Dave Robicheaux, muses on the solitary nature of alcoholic dependence. It's a theme I've picked upon before, maybe driven by those years working at distance from home, where I too have eaten and drunk on my own as the years fade. Makes you think, I guess...

Food on a plate, untouched, congealing, cold,

a knife and fork, unwrapped, lay clean and sterile

beside a creased paper napkin.

Empty tumblers, drained, sticky at the rim,

stack up on the table

as a waitress hands over another shot.

At a certain time of night

the only way to get another drink

is to feign interest in something easy,

something served on a bed of rice.

The waitress seems older than I remember,

older than they used to be.

They don't send the pretty ones to deal

with the ritual inhabitants

of the insomniac booths.

Age is immaterial though,

now that all of the girls

look right through me.

It used to be different.

Once it was subtle, alive,

sometime in the way back,

when they looked at me

instead of through me

with an obvious sense of disinterest.

Another sip, another burn, another cigarette,

and so, the unravelling of my DNA advances,

turning me invisible.

AS OLD AS GEOFFREY BOYCOTT

*Getting older is clearly a theme among these pieces and this is
another poem that touches on that subject, particularly on the fact
that we forget that we were young once and that we were the
'yobs' that older people tutted about or didn't understand. Given
that a few more years have passed in putting this collection
together, I find myself working hard now to remember who I was
so that I might avoid those fears and resentments.*

Hot summers when it never rained,

the grass at the Rec worn away in goal mouths

by size six football boots carried home

in a Woolies paper bag,

milk crate towers in dens in the woods

at the back of the new housing estate,

the Oxhey boys, stone fights,

making up stories about your bruises,

bikes, playing cards in spokes,

being Geoffrey Boycott down in the alley,

finding hiding places in buddleias

and spying on girls on swings.

Second childhood, time to spare,

a mac over your arm in July just in case,

keeping to the path,

bloody hooligans making noise,

vandalism, hoodies, knives and guns,

Victorian values and arthritic knees,

feeling as old as Geoffrey Boycott,

and the alley is blind, a darkness,

full of brooding branches,

muggers and cut throats,

littered with copies of the Mail

blowing on the winds

of too much bloody change.

DEATH OF A COMIC

I read an article about George Carlin, to whom this piece was loosely dedicated, and I fell in love with the idea of an old comic dying, metaphorically and literally, on stage. This piece directly influenced the opening of my first novel, Songs Of Bliss, and the character Ted Line.

"If someone with multiple personalities threatens to kill himself,

is it considered a hostage situation?"

Polite laughter,

sweaty armpits,

shiny suit,

spotlight,

working the floor.

"What if there were no hypothetical questions?"

One liners,

two timing,

three drinks

before curtain up

four seconds of silence.

"The main reason Santa is so jolly

is because he knows where all the bad girls live."

Life after television,

household waste,

cabaret cannon fodder,

mile after mile,

club after club.

"If God dropped acid, would he see people?"

Mine's a double,

don't mind if I do,

B&B conversations,

appreciative audiences,

the good old days.

"Isn't it a bit unnerving that doctors call what they do 'practice'?"

Filling,

warming up,

could have been

a contender,

dying at the end of the pier.

"One tequila, two tequila, three tequila, floor."

(with thanks to George Carlin)

FALLING IN LOVE WITH EMMA PEEL

This is a love poem. We've met Mollie, my maternal grandmother, and this piece is about Pop. Arnold Grice Carter is still with me in thought and artefact. To this day I use his switchblade pocket knife when gardening. Pop was a bear of a man, laying patios single - handedly well into his seventies, and a huge influence on who I have become.

Before colour television,

which wasn't natural,

the make do and mend decades

were measured by coat hangers.

After ten years of good use

the suit from Moss Bros,

fabric for high days,

for charabanc and trolley days,

slid down the rail, second best,

and second went to the allotment,

patched and creosote stained.

When I began to know him,

to store him in my solid state,

he only ever wore gardening,

and on a Saturday afternoon

he drank medicinal brandies,

thumping the arm rest, shouting

at Jackie Pallo and Mick McManus.

He was solid in monochrome,

immortal, locked in thrift, quiet,

unsinkable, but most importantly, mine,

and as a treat on Friday nights,

him in his chair and me on the rug,

we'd share Edam and Marmite on Ryvita

watching Emma Peel high kick

her way into our childish hearts.

WIND SHEAR

A late night down on the farm, solitary, keeping the Aga stoked while Karen slept through the ravages of chemotherapy. This piece was probably tinged with Pinot, an attempt to describe navigation across choppy waters....

Bottoming a surge wave, spume drenched,

lashed to the bow seat, skin tight,

salt bleached, facing a cold war wall of water,

sucked into the barrel, rising,

cresting a spitting cobra's dripping fangs,

this ripped and torn shell of a boat

launches herself across a smothering grey mist

on a barracking ocean, and blind

in the roaring dark, we hit something solid

at the height of the storm.

A hand on my arm, a grasping embrace,

waist deep, a breath on my cheek,

a word screamed at me that flies away

on the shear, and then a head falls,

buried in the sodden hair of my chest,

and we cling for dear life to the mane

of this serpent sea, the two of us,

rowlock bound, afraid to look for any horizon

beyond the fringe of an eyelid,

riding out Lear's flying storm.

We remain flotsam until,

broken down with fatigue, cramped and stiff,

on a swell subsiding, under a warming sun,

our bones heal, our fingers unbend,

and the heavy, blackened wood at our feet dries.

We relax our grip on one another,

drifting on a sunbeam, away, apart, unnamed,

alone but for that last look into her eyes

in this endless dream of a perfect storm.

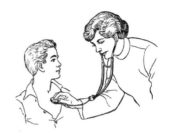

C.T.

An attempt, I think, to make sense of the feelings aroused by the seemingly endless round of cancer treatments. There are a range of conflicts inherent in living with cancer. There is guilt, a sense of impotence, of wonder at the strength of the woman fighting, of anger... you don't actually understand how you are supposed to behave, and you fear your weaknesses...

Lights are going out

behind twitching curtains

drawn across windows,

but a sliver of grey-black

curiosity betrays those ever present,

eagerly nervous voyeurs.

A fire burns a shadow play,

a flickering half-life tale,

where splintered wood lifts

in feathered flight beneath

staccato stone-calls on concrete,

the sound of a hail of silver bullets

hitting the werecell

but disintegrating, falling to dust

in the fire's draw, crackling,

and here, on a rising blister

of pockmarked tarmac,

the one obvious spectator,

I can feel heat sting my skin

before the baton charge.

Towers of glass stand

black and dull and shattered,

ground zero chokes,

is looted by muffled boys

trailing severed veins

of cable blue across

the city's paved flesh.

The electron shot, wide eyed,

pans out, moving left field,

and one by one the streets fade

into the inky headline banner news,

a cartoon grotesque, a tracing,

the colour-code, a digitally

interpreted image that describes

an oily film, softly organic,

a two-dimensional biosphere,

through which a black tidal bore

rides curves and contours,

scouring the bones clean,

infecting the city's liver.

This scan is a map, a web

of dark and urgent matter,

hot spots, a riot in the urban jungle,

and this voice at the edge is mine.

I am standing on the city's risen skin

listening to the beat

of blunt wood on riot shields,

watching young kids scatter

home to their mothers,

before the rising tide hits home,

an inevitable sea of tears

boiling at their heels.

She is, this city of mine,

the hearth of kin,

turned out from within,

exposed, a ferocious,

cornered mother with cubs,

and I am a watchman,

stone, the ever-reluctant stoic

in the face of the diagnostic.

CINDERELLA IN THE PARK

A difficult piece, this one. After Karen died I took a little comfort where I could and this piece relates to that. I have very mixed feelings about that period and my responses to things like loneliness, guilt, anger and the like. It was a necessarily broken time, but hopeful, I believe, even if, at the time, I was an unreliable man.

She starts the ball rolling with a binary word,

a promissory note of a moment in time

redeemable with a kiss, and released from the cinders

she walks across lightly scented

harvest grass begging for strings and a crying song.

There is no mouse-horse harness pulled tight,

nor can any ratty coachman be seen

whipping the afternoon along at a frenzy,

but over by the far chain fence

lizard tongued footmen loll against a tree.

She sits under a white shiplap pavilion clock

dressed in the frill and spill of anticipation,

dreaming of his pink lips at her neck,

of his hands caressing her naked arms,

and she kicks off a threadbare mule

to feel the cool juice of crushed blades

between her toes, to taste the rising stain

of man on her tongue. She colours

at the sound of footsteps, turns towards

a low burning sun, and squints as she smiles.

A blending of skin. Time travels by the surge

of blood unleashed by the warmth of his breath.

Her card is marked and her dances taken.

Her skin is pricked by his urgent fingers and she

waltzes life away to the fiddles reeling in her head

until the clock hands above her spin out past

the midnight bell, the run-home naked time,

when her rags and hanging mules assume the dull

shades of autumn hearths as she greets those

who call her wife and mother with a broom in her hand.

KILLING TIME

Another cancer piece. Writing was catharsis, a way of exorcising the sense of personal futility in the world, a way of marshalling those troubles and finding a moment of peace in which to strengthen my resolve. Writing was also a way to celebrate the sheer and utter brilliance of the woman at the heart of everything.

Cuban heels on a linoleum floor, machine buffed,

deeply cleansed to avoid measly infections,

in cases of emergency scratch and sniff;

antiseptic spirits mingling with the metallic smell

of blood, a backdrop, a roughly painted box-set,

upon which I tap-dance every third Tuesday,

and then sit busy with a crossword

amongst the bonnets and bloody eruptions,

a sea of labouring skin, waiting for her,

killing time.

I wake with the morning scratch, duvet snug,

and next to me she tries to open her eyes

but her lids are glued shut, side-effects,

and her bones ache with the growing of new life.

She drips daily away, tiring visibly,

so much effort spent in staying with me

that her skin shifts in transparent waves,

but she tries to smile away the pain,

surfacing slowly, waiting out the storm,

killing time.

A cycle of life, a triumvirate passage

of symptomatic markers, a succession

of phased decay that leeches into the walls,

a home of hopes and dreams where now

doors shut firmly against a winter's bleak light,

and so we hunker down, and I dare not look

in the mirror when the bathroom door is locked

in case I see a reflection from a caring soul,

a shadow man, a face so tired of waiting,

of draining down in the killing time.

SHEER ACT OF WILL

If the last piece was introspective and maybe even a cry of pain, this was a counterpoint written very soon after Killing Time. Where Killing Time is a reflection of the despair and tiredness inherent in the cancer process, Sheer Act Of Will is the absolute celebration of the woman at the heart of it all.

Pathologically determined to intemperate decay

she takes a toiling step on a staircase,

up into the highland heathers of soft furnishings,

pausing to keep the spin of the world at bay,

holding the rail, a guide to the perpendicular

progress of Sunday morning shopping,

a day when the slowing of the crowd

mitigates her own dull pulse.

She breathes deeply, takes another step,

and finding her head level with the base units

of floral displays, seeing the object

of a laissez-faire desire, she wills her legs

to carry her steroidal body this final lap

into a retail stratosphere.

With a beeline made to the roll-up rugs,

to the colour swatch and the regimentally

distressed leather sofas, she sits

and with a nonchalant hand

shrugs away the price tags.

The colour supplement advert is a sham.

Promised discounts don't apply

to the one floor covering she likes.

I wait while she gathers herself,

looks at a notebook and determines

the shortest route to a new-born child's slippers.

I stop again at the foot of the stairs

and turn and look back at her

as she makes an effort, makes light

of the labours of her day with a deeply etched smile.

I wish on a thousand starry Gods

that we could travel backwards,

up through time, instead of making

this inevitable gravitational descent.

ABOUT THE AUTHOR

I was born in 1962 into a predominantly sporting household – Dad being a good footballer, playing senior amateur and lower league professional football in England, as well as running a series of private businesses in partnership with mum, herself an accomplished and medal winning dancer.

I obtained a degree in History from Leeds University before wandering rather haphazardly into the emerging world of business computing in the late nineteen-eighties.

A little like my sporting father, I followed a succession of amateur writing paths alongside my career in technology, including working as a freelance journalist and book reviewer, my one claim to fame being a by-line in a national newspaper in the UK, The Sunday people.

I also spent 10 years treading the boards, appearing all over the south of the UK in pantos and plays, in village halls and occasionally on the stage of a professional theatre or two.

Following the sporting theme, and a while after I hung up my own boots, I worked on live TV broadcasts for the BBC, ITV, TVNZ, EuroSport and others as a rugby "Stato", covering Heineken Cups,

Six Nations, IRB World Sevens and IRB World Cups in the late '90's and early '00's.

I try to combine my love of storytelling with a passion for information technology, working as a senior leader and investor in technology based businesses.

You can find out more about me at: www.boyonabench.com

SOLITUDE

ALSO BY CLIVE GILSON - *FICTION*

- Songs Of Bliss
- The Mechanic's Curse
- The Insomniac Booth
- A Solitude Of Stars

AS EDITOR – *FIRESIDE TALES – Part 1, Europe*

- Tales From The Land Of Dragons
- Tales From The Land Of The Brave
- Tales From The Land Of Saints And Scholars
- Tales From The Land Of Hope And Glory
- Tales From Lands Of Snow And Ice
- Tales From The Viking Isles
- Tales From The Forest Lands
- Tales From The Old Norse
- More Tales About Saints And Scholars
- More Tales About Hope And Glory
- More Tales About Snow And Ice
- Tales From The Land Of Rabbits
- Tales Told By Bulls And Wolves
- Tales Of Fire & Bronze
- Tales From The Land Of The Strigoi
- Tales Told By The Wind Mother
- Tales From Gallia
- Tales From Germania

EDITOR – *FIRESIDE TALES – Part 2, North America*

- Okaraxta - Tales From The Great Plains
- Tibik-Kìzis – Tales From The Great Lakes & Canada
- Jóhonaa'éí –Tales From America's South West
- Qugaaĝix̂ - First Nation Tales From Alaska & The Arctic
- Karahkwa - First Nation Tales From America's Eastern States
- Pot-Likker - Folklore, Fairy Tales and Settler Stories From America

IMAGE ACKNOWLEDGEMENTS:

- Cover, Marbha @ Pixabay
- Frontispiece, Open Clipart Vectors @ Pixabay
- Preface, Open Clipart Vectors @ Pixabay
- Arif's Legs, Marina Westerkamp @ Pixabay
- At One Blow, Mohammed Hassan @ Pixabay
- Balancing Mixed Vegetables on A Motorway Bridge, Prawny @ Pixabay
- Burning Books, Muhib @ Pixabay
- Courtyard, Open Clipart Vectors @ Pixabay
- Ghost Lies in Light, Gordon Johnson @ Pixabay
- Hesperus Wrecked, Gordon Johnson @ Pixabay
- Lena's Parting Gifts, Pandanna Imagen @ Pixabay
- Mollie Smokes Players, Open Clipart Vectors @ Pixabay
- Roses Remembered, Open Clipart Vectors @ Pixabay
- The Man Who Loves Comets, Gordon Johnson @ Pixabay
- Angel Falls, Gordon Johnson @ Pixabay
- Llanarrow, Clker-Free-Vector-Images @ Pixabay
- A Broken Heart, Open Clipart Vectors @ Pixabay
- Blind Man Bathing, Gordon Johnson @ Pixabay
- Boys in Summer, Mohammed Hassan @ Pixabay
- Chairs Remember Too, Clker-Free-Vector-Images @ Pixabay
- Closing of the Chapel, Gordon Johnson @ Pixabay
- In for The Kill, Clker-Free-Vector-Images @ Pixabay
- Into the Walled Garden, Gordon Johnson @ Pixabay
- Let's All Move to France, B0red @ Pixabay
- Miss You, Clker-Free-Vector-Images @ Pixabay
- Out of The Walled Garden, Gordon Johnson @ Pixabay
- The Colour of Her Eyes, Prettysleepy1 @ Pixabay
- Screaming At The Sea, Clker-Free-Vector-Images @ Pixabay
- Highford Winter, Gordon Johnson @ Pixabay
- Seven of Eight, Stux @ Pixabay
- Words Fail Me, An Le Bao @ Pixabay
- Blessed by the Moon's Blush, Open Clipart Vectors @ Pixabay
- Evidence of Sleep, Open Clipart Vectors @ Pixabay
- Our Lady of Silence, Open Clipart Vectors @ Pixabay
- Why the Dog Goes Early to Bed..., Clker-Free-Vector-Images @ Pixabay
- Cold Shore Ballad, Clker-Free-Vector-Images @ Pixabay
- For the Long Down Road, Open Clipart Vectors @ Pixabay
- John, Terrorist, Open Clipart Vectors @ Pixabay
- Princess of the Western World, Gordon Johnson @ Pixabay
- The Man with the Snake Oil Tongue, Open Clipart Vectors @ Pixabay
- Boy Comes Home, Open Clipart Vectors @ Pixabay
- Butterfly, Open Clipart Vectors @ Pixabay
- Haversham, Gordon Johnson @ Pixabay
- A Short History of Old Buildings, Gordon Johnson @ Pixabay
- Cancer Ward, 2998800 @ Pixabay
- Dirty Tumours, McMurryJulie @ Pixabay
- Explorer 242, Clker-Free-Vector-Images @ Pixabay
- Quiet Time in a Crowd, Clker-Free-Vector-Images @ Pixabay
- Little Black Rain Cloud, Clker-Free-Vector-Images @ Pixabay
- On the Doorstep, Open Clipart Vectors @ Pixabay
- Short-sighted Bees, Open Clipart Vectors @ Pixabay

Out Of The Walled Garden

- The Insomniac Booth, Clker-Free-Vector-Images @ Pixabay
- As Old as Geoffrey Boycott, Open Clipart Vectors @ Pixabay
- Death of a Comic, Clker-Free-Vector-Images @ Pixabay
- Falling in Love with Emma Peel, Mohamed Hassan @ Pixabay
- Wind Shear, Open Clipart Vectors @ Pixabay
- C.T., Clker-Free-Vector-Images @ Pixabay
- Cinderella in the Park, Mohamed Hassan @ Pixabay
- Killing Time, BedexpStock @ Pixabay
- Sheer Act of Will, Mohamed Hassan @ Pixabay

CPSIA information can be obtained
at www.ICGtesting.com
Printed in the USA
BVHW031756281220
596587BV00005B/31

9 781913 500382